Tam o'Shanter

ROBERT BURNS

A Phoenix Paperback

This abridged edition published in 1996 by Phoenix
a division of Orion Books Ltd
Orion House, 5 Upper St Martin's Lane, London WC2H 9EA

Copyright © Orion Books Ltd 1996

ISBN 1 85799 659 3

Typeset by Deltatype Ltd, Ellesmere Port, Cheshire
Printed and bound in Great Britain by
Clays Ltd, St Ives plc

CONTENTS

John Barleycorn. A Ballad

1

There was three kings into the east,
　　Three kings both great and high,
And they hae sworn a solemn oath
　　John Barleycorn should die.

2

They took a plough and plough'd him down,
　　Put clods upon his head,
And they hae sworn a solemn oath
　　John Barleycorn was dead.

3

But the chearful Spring came kindly on,
　　And show'rs began to fall;
John Barleycorn got up again,
　　And sore surpris'd them all.

4

The sultry suns of Summer came,
　　And he grew thick and strong,
His head weel arm'd wi' pointed spears,
　　That no one should him wrong.

5

The sober Autumn enter'd mild,
  When he grew wan and pale;
His bending joints and drooping head
  Show'd he began to fail.

6

His colour sicken'd more and more,
  He faded into age;
And then his enemies began
  To show their deadly rage.

7

They've taen a weapon, long and sharp,
  And cut him by the knee;
They ty'd him fast upon a cart,
  Like a rogue for forgerie.

8

They laid him down upon his back,
  And cudgell'd him full sore;
They hung him up before the storm,
  And turn'd him o'er and o'er.

9

They filled up a darksome pit
  With water to the brim,
They heaved in John Barleycorn,
  There let him sink or swim.

10

They laid him out upon the floor,
　　To work him farther woe,
And still, as signs of life appear'd,
　　They toss'd him to and fro.

11

They wasted, o'er a scorching flame,
　　The marrow of his bones;
But a Miller us'd him worst of all,
　　For he crush'd him between two stones.

12

And they hae taen his very heart's blood,
　　And drank it round and round;
And still the more and more they drank,
　　Their joy did more abound.

13

John Barleycorn was a hero bold,
　　Of noble enterprise,
For if you do but taste his blood,
　　'Twill make your courage rise.

'Twill make a man forget his woe;
   'Twill heighten all his joy:
'Twill make the widow's heart to sing,
   Tho' the tear were in her eye.

15

Then let us toast John Barleycorn,
   Each man a glass in hand;
And may his great posterity
   Ne'er fail in old Scotland!

*To a Mouse, On turning her up in her Nest,
with the Plough, November, 1785*

Wee, sleeket, cowran, tim'rous *beastie*,
O, what a panic 's in thy breastie!
Thou need na start awa sae hasty,
     Wi' bickering brattle!
I wad be laith to rin an' chase thee,
     Wi' murd'ring *pattle*!

I'm truly sorry Man's dominion
Has broken Nature's social union,
An' justifies that ill opinion,
     Which makes thee startle,

At me, poor earth-born companion,
             An' *fellow-mortal*!

I doubt na, whyles, but thou may *thieve*;
What then? poor beastie, thou maun live!
A *daimen-icker* in a *thrave*
             'S a sma' request:
I'll get a blessin wi' the lave,
             An' never miss't!

Thy wee-bit *housie*, too, in ruin!
It's silly wa's the win's are strewin!
An' naething, now, to big a new ane,
             O' foggage green!
An' bleak *December's winds* ensuin,
             Baith snell an' keen!

Thou saw the fields laid bare an' wast,
An' weary *Winter* comin fast,
An' cozie here, beneath the blast,
             Thou thought to dwell,
Till crash! the cruel *coulter* past
             Out thro' thy cell.

That wee-bit heap o' leaves an' stibble,
Has cost thee monie a weary nibble!
Now thou's turn'd out, for a' thy trouble,
             But house or hald,

To thole the Winter's *sleety dribble*,
        An' *cranreuch* cauld!

But Mousie, thou art no thy-lane,
In proving *foresight* may be vain:
The best laid schemes o' *Mice* an' *Men*,
        Gang aft agley,
An' lea'e us nought but grief an' pain,
        For promis'd joy!

Still, thou art blest, compar'd wi' *me*!
The *present* only toucheth thee:
But Och! I *backward* cast my e'e,
        On prospects drear!
An' *forward*, tho' I canna *see*,
        I *guess* an' *fear*!

The Twa Dogs. A Tale

'Twas in that place o' *Scotland*'s isle,
That bears the name o' auld king COIL,
Upon a bonie day in June,
When wearing thro' the afternoon
Twa Dogs, that were na thrang at hame,
Forgather'd ance upon a time.

    The first I'll name, they ca'd him *Ceasar*,
Was keepet for his Honor's pleasure;

His hair, his size, his mouth, his lugs,
Show'd he was nane o' Scotland's dogs;
But whalpet some place far abroad,
Where sailors gang to fish for Cod.

His locked, letter'd, braw brass-collar,
Show'd him the *gentleman* an' *scholar*;
But tho' he was o' high degree,
The fient a pride na pride had he,
But wad hae spent an hour caressan,
Ev'n wi' a Tinkler-gipsey's *messan*:
At *Kirk* or *Market, Mill* or *Smiddie*;
Nae tawtied *tyke*, tho' e'er sae duddie,
But he wad stan't, as glad to see him,
An' stroan't on stanes an' hillocks wi' him.

The tither was a *ploughman's collie*,
A rhyming, ranting, raving billie,
Wha for his friend an' comrade had him,
And in his freaks had *Luath* ca'd him;
After some dog in *Highlan Sang*,
Was made lang syne, lord knows how lang.

He was a gash an' faithfu' *tyke*,
As ever lap a sheugh, or dyke!
His honest sonsie, baws'nt *face*,
Ay gat him friends in ilka place;
His *breast* was white, his towzie *back*,

Weel clad wi' coat o' glossy black;
His gawsie tail, wi' upward curl,
Hung owre his hurdies wi' a swirl.

Nae doubt but they were fain o' ither,
An' unco pack an' thick the gither;
Wi' social *nose* whyles snuff'd an' snowcket;
Whyles mice an' modewurks they howcket;
Whyles scour'd awa in lang excursion,
An' worry'd ither in *diversion*;
Untill wi' daffin weary grown,
Upon a knowe they sat them down,
An' there began a lang digression
About the *lords o' the creation*.

CEASAR

I've aften wonder'd, honest *Luath*,
What sort o' life poor dogs like you have;
An' when the *gentry's* life I saw,
What way *poor bodies* liv'd ava.

Our *Laird* gets in his racked rents,
His coals, his kane, an' a' his stents;
He rises when he likes himsel;
His flunkies answer at the bell;
He ca's his coach; he ca's his horse;
He draws a bonie, silken purse

As lang's my *tail*, whare thro' the steeks,
The yellow, letter'd *Geordie* keeks.

    Frae morn to een it's nought but toiling,
At baking, roasting, frying, boiling:
An' tho' the gentry first are steghan,
Yet ev'n the *ha' folk* fill their peghan
Wi' sauce, ragouts, an' sic like trashtrie,
That 's little short o' downright wastrie.
Our *Whipper-in*, wee, blastiet wonner,
Poor, worthless elf, it eats a dinner,
Better than only *Tenant-man*
His Honor has in a' the lan':
An' what poor *Cot-folk* pit their painch in,
I own it 's past my comprehension. –

LUATH

    Trowth, *Ceasar*, whyles they're fash'd eneugh;
A *Cotter* howckan in a sheugh,
Wi' dirty stanes biggan an dyke,
Bairan a quarry, an' sic like,
Himsel, a wife, he thus sustains,
A smytrie o' wee, duddie weans,
An' nought but his han'-daurk, to keep
Them right an' tight in *thack an' raep*.

    An' when they meet wi' sair disasters,
Like loss o' health, or want o' masters,

9

Ye maist wad think, a wee touch langer,
An' they maun starve o' cauld an' hunger:
But how it comes, I never kent yet,
They're maistly wonderfu' contented;
An' buirdly chiels, an' clever hizzies,
Are bred in sic a way as this is.

CEASAR

But then, to see how ye're negleket,
How huff'd, an' cuff'd, an' disrespeket!
L—d man, our gentry care as little
For *delvers, ditchers*, an' sic cattle;
They gang as saucy by poor folk,
As I wad by a stinkan brock.

I've notic'd, on our Laird's *court-day*,
An' mony a time my heart's been wae,
Poor *tenant-bodies*, scant o' cash,
How they maun thole a *factor*'s snash;
He'll stamp an' threaten, curse an' swear,
He'll *apprehend* them, *poind* their gear,
While they maun stand, wi' aspect humble,
An' hear it a', an' fear an' tremble!

I see how folk live that hae riches,
But surely poor-folk maun be *wretches*!

LUATH

They're no sae wretched 's ane wad think;
Tho' constantly on poortith's brink,

They're sae accustom'd wi' the sight,
The view o't gies them little fright.

Then chance an' fortune are sae guided,
They're ay in less or mair provided;
An' tho' fatigu'd wi' close employment,
A blink o' rest 's a sweet enjoyment.

The dearest comfort o' their lives,
Their grushie weans, an' faithfu' wives;
The *prattling things* are just their pride,
That sweetens a' their fire-side.

An' whyles, twalpennie-worth o' *nappy*
Can mak the bodies unco happy;
They lay aside their private cares,
To mind the Kirk an' State affairs;
They'll talk o' *patronage* an' *priests*,
Wi' kindling fury i' their breasts,
Or tell what new taxation's comin,
An' ferlie at the folk in LON'ON.

As bleak-fac'd Hallowmass returns,
They get the jovial, rantan *Kirns*,
When *rural life*, of ev'ry station,
Unite in common recreation;
Love blinks, Wit slaps, an' social Mirth
Forgets there's *care* upo' the earth.

That *merry day* the year begins,
They bar the door on frosty win's;
The nappy reeks wi' mantling ream,
An' sheds a heart-inspiring steam;
The luntan pipe, an' sneeshin mill,
Are handed round wi' right guid will;
The cantie, auld folks, crackan crouse,
The young anes rantan thro' the house –
My heart has been sae fain to see them,
That I for joy hae *barket* wi' them.

Still it's owre true that ye hae said,
Sic game is now owre aften play'd;
There 's monie a creditable *stock*
O' decent, honest, fawsont folk,
Are riven out baith root an' branch,
Some rascal's pridefu' greed to quench,
Wha thinks to knit himsel the faster
In favor wi' some *gentle Master*,
Wha, aiblins, thrang a *parliamentin*,
For *Britain's guid* his saul indentin –

CEASAR

Haith lad, ye little ken about it;
For Britain's guid! guid faith! I doubt it.
Say rather, gaun as PREMIERS lead him,
An' saying *aye* or *no* 's they bid him:

At Operas an' Plays parading,

Mortgaging, gambling, masquerading:
Or maybe, in a frolic daft,
To HAGUE or CALAIS takes a waft,
To make a *tour* an' take a whirl,
To learn *bon ton* an' see the worl'.

There, at VIENNA or VERSAILLES,
He rives his father's auld entails;
Or by MADRID he takes the rout,
To thrum *guittarres* an' fecht wi' *nowt*;
Or down *Italian Vista* startles,
Wh-re-hunting amang groves o' myrtles:
Then bowses drumlie *German-water*,
To make himsel look fair an' fatter,
An' clear the consequential sorrows,
Love-gifts of Carnival Signioras.
For Britain's guid! for her destruction!
Wi' dissipation, feud an' faction!

LUATH
Hech man! dear sirs! is that the gate,
They waste sae mony a braw estate!
Are we sae foughten an' harass'd
For gear to gang that gate at last!

O would they stay aback frae courts,
An' please themsels wi' countra sports,
It wad for ev'ry ane be better,

The *Laird*, the *Tenant*, an' the *Cotter*!
For thae frank, rantan, ramblan billies,
Fient haet o' them's illhearted fellows;
Except for breakin o' their timmer,
Or speakin lightly o' their *Limmer*;
Or shootin of a hare or moorcock,
The ne'er-a-bit they're ill to poor folk.

But will ye tell me, master *Cesar*,
Sure *great folk* 's life's a life o' pleasure?
Nae cauld nor hunger e'er can steer them,
The vera thought o't need na fear them.

CAESAR
L—d man, were ye but whyles where I am,
The *gentles* ye wad ne'er envy them!

It's true, they needna starve or sweat,
Thro' Winter's cauld, or Summer's heat;
They've nae sair-wark to craze their banes,
An' fill *auld-age* wi' grips an' granes:
But *human-bodies* are sic fools,
For a' their Colledges an' Schools,
That when nae *real* ills perplex them,
They *mak* enow themsels to vex them;
An' ay the less they hae to sturt them,
In like proportion, less will hurt them.

A country fellow at the pleugh,
His *acre*'s till'd, he's right eneugh;
A country girl at her wheel,
Her *dizzen*'s done, she's unco weel;
But Gentlemen, an' Ladies warst,
Wi ev'n down *want o' work* they're curst.
They loiter, lounging, lank an' lazy;
Tho' deli-haet ails them, yet uneasy;
Their days, insipid, dull an' tasteless,
Their nights, unquiet, lang an' restless.

An' ev'n their sports, their balls an' races,
Their galloping thro' public places,
There's sic parade, sic pomp an' art,
The joy can scarcely reach the heart.

The *Men* cast out in *party-matches*,
Then sowther a' in deep debauches.
Ae night, they're mad wi' drink an' wh–ring.
Niest day their life is past enduring.

The *Ladies* arm-in-arm in clusters,
As great an' gracious a' as sisters;
But hear their *absent thoughts* o' ither,
They're a' run-deils an' jads the gither
Whyles, owre the wee bit cup an' platie,
They sip the *scandal-potion* pretty;
Or lee-lang nights, wi' crabbet leuks,

15

Pore owre the devil's *pictur'd beuks*;
Stake on a chance a farmer's stackyard.
An' cheat like ony *unhang'd blackguard*.

There 's some exceptions, man an' woman;
But this is Gentry's life in common.

By this, the sun was out o' sight,
An' darker gloamin brought the night:
The *bum-clock* humm'd wi' lazy drone,
The kye stood rowtan i' the loan;
When up they gat, an' shook their lugs,
Rejoic'd they were na *men* but *dogs*;
An' each took off his several way,
Resolv'd to meet some ither day.

A Fragment – Green grow the rashes O

CHORUS

Green grow the rashes O,
Green grow the rashes O,
The lasses they hae wimble bores,
The widows they hae gashes O.

1

In sober hours I am a priest;
    A hero when I'm tipsey, O;

But I'm a king and ev'ry thing,
    When wi' a wanton Gipsey, O.
        Green grow &c.

2

'Twas late yestreen I met wi' ane,
    An' wow, but she was gentle, O!
Ae han' she pat roun' my cravat,
    The tither to my p— O.
        Green grow &c.

1

I dought na speak – yet was na fley'd –
    My heart play'd duntie, duntie, O;
An' ceremony laid aside,
    I fairly fun' her c-ntie, O. –
        Green grow &c.

To a Haggis

Fair fa' your honest, sonsie face,
Great Chieftan o' the Puddin-race!
Aboon them a' ye tak your place,
                Painch, tripe, or thairm:
Weel are ye wordy of a *grace*
                As lang 's my arm.

The groaning trencher there ye fill,
Your hurdies like a distant hill,
Your *pin* wad help to mend a mill
      In time o' need,
While thro' your pores the dews distil
        Like amber bead.

His knife see Rustic-labour dight,
An' cut you wi' ready slight,
Trenching your gushing entrails bright
      Like onie ditch;
And then, O what a glorious sight,
        Warm-reekin, rich!

Then, horn for horn they stretch an' strive,
Deil tak the hindmost, on they drive,
Till a' their weel-swall'd kytes belyve
      Are bent like drums;
Then auld Guidman, maist like to rive,
        Bethankit hums.

Is there that owre his French *ragout*,
Or *olio* that wad staw a sow,
Or *fricassee* wad mak her spew
      Wi' perfect sconner,
Looks down wi' sneering, scornfu' view
        On sic a dinner?

Poor devil! see him owre his trash,
As feckless as a wither'd rash,
His spindle shank a guid whip-lash,
        His nieve a nit;
Thro' bluidy flood or field to dash,
        O how unfit!

But mark the Rustic, *haggis-fed*,
The trembling earth resounds his tread,
Clap in his walie nieve a blade,
        He'll mak it whissle;
An' legs, an' arms, an' heads will sned,
        Like taps o' thrissle.

Ye Pow'rs wha mak mankind your care,
And dish them out their bill o' fare,
Auld Scotland wants nae skinking ware
        That jaups in luggies;
But, if ye wish her gratefu' pray'r,
        Gie her a *Haggis*!

I love my Jean

Of a' the airts the wind can blaw,
   I dearly like the West;
For there the bony Lassie lives,
   The Lassie I lo'e best:

There's wild-woods grow, and rivers row,
 And mony a hill between;
But day and night my fancy's flight
 Is ever wi' my Jean. –

I see her in the dewy flowers,
 I see her sweet and fair;
I hear her in the tunefu' birds,
 I hear her charm the air:
There's not a bony flower, that springs
 By fountain, shaw, or green;
There's not a bony bird that sings
 But minds me o' my Jean. –

Tam Glen –

My heart is a breaking, dear Tittie,
 Some counsel unto me come len';
To anger them a' is a pity,
 But what will I do wi' Tam Glen? –

I'm thinking, wi' sic a braw fellow,
 In poortith I might mak a fen':
What care I in riches to wallow,
 If I mauna marry Tam Glen. –

There's Lowrie the lard o' Dunmeller,
 'Gude day to you brute' he comes ben:

He brags and he blaws o' his siller,
    But when will he dance like Tam Glen. –

My Minne does constantly deave me,
    And bids me beware o' young men;
They flatter, she says, to deceive me,
    But wha can think sae o' Tam Glen. –

My Daddie says, gin I'll forsake him,
    He'll gie me gude hunder marks ten:
But, if it 's ordain'd I maun take him,
    O wha will I get but Tam Glen?

Yestreen at the Valentines' dealing,
    My heart to my mou gied a sten;
For thrice I drew ane without failing,
    And thrice it was written, Tam Glen. –

The last Halloween I was waukin
    My droukit sark-sleeve, as ye ken;
His likeness cam up the house staukin,
    And the very grey breeks o' Tam Glen!

Come counsel, dear Tittie, don't tarry;
    I'll gie you my bonie black hen,
Gif ye will advise me to Marry
    The lad I lo'e dearly, Tam Glen. –

Auld lang syne

Should auld acquaintance be forgot
   And never brought to mind?
Should auld acquaintance be forgot,
   And auld lang syne!

CHORUS

For auld lang syne, my jo,
   For auld lang syne,
We'll tak a cup o' kindness yet
   For auld syne.

And surely ye'll be your pint stowp!
   And surely I'll be mine!
And we'll take a cup o' kindness yet,
   For auld lang syne.
     For auld, &c.

We twa hae run about the braes,
   And pou'd the gowans fine;
But we've wander'd mony a weary fitt,
   Sin auld lang syne.
     For auld, &c.

We twa hae paidl'd in the burn,
   Frae morning sun till dine;
But seas between us braid hae roar'd,

Sin auld lang syne.
    For auld, &c.

And there's a hand, my trusty fiere!
    And gie's a hand o' thine!
And we'll tak a right gude-willie-waught,
    For auld lang syne.
        For auld, &c.

My bony Mary

Go fetch to me a pint o' wine,
    And fill it in a silver tassie;
That I may drink, before I go,
    A service to my bonie lassie:
The boat rocks at the Pier o' Leith,
    Fu' loud the wind blaws frae the Ferry,
The ship rides by the Berwick-law,
    And I maun leave my bony Mary.

The trumpets sound, the banners fly,
    The glittering spears are ranked ready,
The shouts o' war are heard afar,
    The battle closes deep and bloody.
It's not the roar o' sea or shore,
    Wad make me langer wish to tarry;

Nor shouts o' war that 's heard afar –
It's leaving thee, my bony Mary!

Afton Water

Flow gently, sweet Afton, among thy green braes,
Flow gently, I'll sing thee a song in thy praise;
My Mary's asleep by thy murmuring stream,
Flow gently, sweet Afton, disturb not her dream.

Thou stock dove whose echo resounds thro' the glen,
Ye wild whistling blackbirds in yon thorny den,
Thou green crested lapwing thy screaming forbear,
I charge you disturb not my slumbering Fair.

How lofty, sweet Afton, thy neighbouring hills,
Far mark'd with the courses of clear, winding rills;
There daily I wander as noon rises high,
My flocks and my Mary's sweet Cot in my eye.

How pleasant thy banks and green vallies below,
Where wild in the woodlands the primroses blow;
There oft as mild ev'ning weeps over the lea,
The sweet scented birk shades my Mary and me.

Thy crystal stream, Afton, how lovely it glides,
And winds by the cot where my Mary resides;

How wanton thy waters her snowy feet lave,
As gathering sweet flowerets she stems thy clear wave.

Flow gently, sweet Afton, among thy green braes,
Flow gently, sweet River, the theme of my lays;
My Mary's asleep by thy murmuring stream,
Flow gently, sweet Afton, disturb not her dream.

Willie brew'd a peck o' maut

O Willie brew'd a peck o' maut,
   And Rob and Allan cam to see;
Three blyther hearts, that lee lang night,
   Ye wad na found in Christendie.

CHORUS

We are na fou, we're nae that fou,
   But just a drappie in our e'e;
The cock may craw, the day may daw,
   And ay we'll taste the barley bree.

Here are we met, three merry boys,
   Three merry boys I trow are we;
And mony a night we've merry been,
   And mony mae we hope to be!
      We are na fou, &c.

It is the moon, I ken her horn,
    That's blinkin in the lift sae hie;
She shines sae bright to wyle us hame,
    But by my sooth she'll wait a wee!
      We are na fou, &c.

Wha first shall rise to gang awa,
    A cuckold, coward loun is he!
Wha first beside his chair shall fa',
He is the king amang us three!
      We are na fou, &c.

My love she's but a lassie yet –

My love she's but a lassie yet;
My love she's but a lassie yet;
We'll let her stand a year or twa,
    She'll no be half sae saucy yet. –

I rue the day I sought her O,
I rue the day I sought her O,
Wha gets her needs na say he's woo'd,
    But he may say he's brought her O. –

Come draw a drap o' the best o't yet,
Come draw a drap o' the best o't yet:
Gae seek for Pleasure whare ye will,
    But here I never misst it yet. –

We're a' dry wi' drinking o't,
We're a' dry wi' drinking o't:
The minister kisst the fidler's wife,
    He could na preach for thinkin o't. –

My heart 's in the Highlands

My heart 's in the Highlands, my heart is not here;
My heart 's in the Highlands a chasing the deer;
Chasing the wild deer, and following the roe;
My heart 's in the Highlands, wherever I go. –

Farewell to the Highlands, farewell to the North;
The birth-place of Valour, the country of Worth:
Wherever I wander, wherever I rove,
The hills of the Highlands for ever I love. –

Farewell to the mountains high cover'd with snow;
Farewell to the Straths and green vallies below:
Farewell to the forests and wild-hanging woods;
Farewell to the torrents and loud-pouring floods. –

My heart 's in the Highlands, my heart is not here,
My heart 's in the Highlands, a chasing the deer:
Chasing the wild deer, and following the roe;
My heart 's in the Highlands, wherever I go. –

John Anderson my Jo

John Anderson my jo, John,
    When we were first acquent;
Your locks were like the raven,
    Your bony brow was brent;
But now your brow is beld, John,
    Your locks are like the snaw;
But blessings on your frosty pow,
    John Anderson my Jo.

John Anderson my jo, John,
    We clamb the hill the gither;
And mony a canty day, John,
    We've had wi' ane anither:
Now we maun totter down, John,
    And hand in hand we'll go;
And sleep the gither at the foot,
    John Anderson my Jo.

Tam o' Shanter. A Tale

Of Brownyis and of Bogillis full is this buke.

GAWIN DOUGLAS

When chapman billies leave the street,
And drouthy neebors, neebors meet,

As market-days are wearing late,
An' folk begin to tak the gate;
While we sit bousing at the nappy,
And getting fou and unco happy,
We think na on the lang Scots miles,
The mosses, waters, slaps, and styles,
That lie between us and our hame,
Whare sits our sulky sullen dame,
Gathering her brows like gathering storm,
Nursing her wrath to keep it warm.

   This truth fand honest *Tam o' Shanter*,
As he frae Ayr ae night did canter,
(Auld Ayr, wham ne'er a town surpasses,
For honest men and bonny lasses.)

   O *Tam*! hadn't thou but been sae wise,
As ta'en thy ain wife *Kate*'s advice!
She tauld thee weel thou was a skellum,
A blethering, blustering, drunken blellum;
That frae November till October,
Ae market-day thou was nae sober;
That ilka melder, wi' the miller,
Thou sat as lang as thou had siller;
That every naig was ca'd a shoe on,
The smith and thee gat roaring fou on;
That at the L–d's house, even on Sunday,
Thou drank wi' Kirkton Jean till Monday.

She prophesied that late or soon,
Thou would be found deep drown'd in Doon;
Or catch'd wi' warlocks in the mirk,
By *Alloway*'s auld haunted kirk.

Ah, gentle dames! it gars me greet,
To think how mony counsels sweet,
How mony lengthen'd sage advices,
The husband frae the wife despises!

But to our tale: Ae market-night,
Tam had got planted unco right;
Fast by an ingle, bleezing finely,
Wi' reaming swats, that drank divinely;
And at his elbow, Souter *Johnny*,
His ancient, trusty, drouthy crony;
Tam lo'ed him like a vera brither;
They had seen fou for weeks thegither.
The night drave on wi' sangs and clatter;
And ay the ale was growing better:
The landlady and *Tam* grew gracious,
Wi' favours, secret, sweet, and precious:
The Souter tauld his queerest stories;
The landlord's laugh was ready chorus:
The storm without might rair and rustle,
Tam did na mind the storm a whistle.

Care, mad to see a man sae happy,
E'en drown'd himsel amang the nappy:

As bees flee hame wi' lades o' treasure,
The minutes wing'd their way wi' pleasure:
Kings may be blest, but *Tam* was glorious,
O'er a' the ills o' life victorious!

But pleasures are like poppies spread,
You seize the flower, its bloom is shed;
Or like the snow falls in the river,
A moment white – then melts for ever;
Or like the borealis race,
That flit ere you can point their place;
Or like the rainbow's lovely form
Evanishing amid the storm. –
Nae man can tether time or tide;
The hour approaches *Tam* maun ride;
That hour, o' night's black arch the key-stane,
That dreary hour he mounts his beast in;
And sic a night he taks the road in,
As ne'er poor sinner was abroad in.

The wind blew as 'twad blawn its last;
The rattling showers rose on the blast;
The speedy gleams the darkness swallow'd;
Loud, deep, and lang, the thunder bellow'd:
That night, a child might understand,
The Deil had business on his hand.

Weel mounted on his gray mare, *Meg*,
A better never lifted leg,

Tam skelpit on thro' dub and mire,
Despising wind, and rain, and fire;
Whiles holding fast his gude blue bonnet;
Whiles crooning o'er some auld Scots sonnet;
Whiles glowring round wi' prudent cares,
Lest bogles catch him unawares:
Kirk-Alloway was drawing nigh,
Whare ghaists and houlets nightly cry. –

By this time he was cross the ford,
Whare, in the snaw, the chapman smoor'd;
And past the birks and meikle stane,
Where drunken *Charlie* brak 's neck-bane;
And thro' the whins, and by the cairn,
Whare hunters fand the murder'd bairn;
And near the thorn, aboon the well,
Whare *Mungo*'s mither hang'd hersel. –
Before him *Doon* pours all his floods;
The doubling storm roars thro' the woods;
The lightnings flash from pole to pole;
Near and more near the thunders roll:
When, glimmering thro' the groaning trees,
Kirk-Alloway seem'd in a bleeze;
Thro' ilka bore the beams were glancing;
And loud resounded mirth and dancing. –

Inspiring bold *John Barleycorn*!

What dangers thou canst make us scorn!

Wi' tippeny, we fear nae evil;
Wi' usquabae, we'll face the devil! –
The swats sae ream'd in *Tammie*'s noddle,
Fair play, he car'd na deils a boddle,
But *Maggie* stood right sair astonish'd,
Till, by the heel and hand admonish'd,
She ventured forward on the light;
And, vow! *Tam* saw an unco sight!
Warlock and witches in a dance;
Nae cotillion brent new frae *France*,
But hornpipes, jigs, strathspeys, and reels,
Put life and mettle in their heels.
A winnock-bunker in the east,
There sat auld Nick, in shape o' beast;
A towzie tyke, black, grim, and large,
To gie them music was his charge:
He screw'd the pipes and gart them skirl,
Till roof and rafters a' did dirl. –
Coffins stood round, like open presses,
That shaw'd the dead in their last dresses;
And by some devilish cantraip slight
Each in its cauld hand held a light. –
By which heroic *Tam* was able
To note upon the haly table,
A murderer's banes in gibbet airns;
Twa span-lang, wee, unchristen'd bairns;
A thief, new-cutted frae a rape,
Wi' his last gasp his gab did gape;

Five tomahawks, wi' blude red-rusted;
Five scymitars, wi' murder crusted;
A garter, which a babe had strangled;
A knife, a father's throat had mangled,
Whom his ain son o' life bereft,
The grey hairs yet stack to the heft;
Wi' mair o' horrible and awefu',
Which even to name wad be unlawfu'.

As *Tammie* glow'rd, amaz'd, and curious,
The mirth and fun grew fast and furious:
The piper loud and louder blew;
The dancers quick and quicker flew;
They reel'd, they set, they cross'd, they cleekit,
Till ilka carlin swat and reekit,
And coost her duddies to the wark,
And linket at it in her sark!

Now, *Tam, O Tam*! had thae been queans,
A' plump and strapping in their teens,
Their sarks, instead o' creeshie flannen,
Been snaw-white seventeen hunder linnen!
Thir breeks o' mine, my only pair,
That ance were plush, o' gude blue hair,
I wad hae gi'en them off my hurdies,
For ae blink o' the bonie burdies!

But wither'd beldams, auld and droll,
Rigwoodie hags wad spean a foal,

Lowping and flinging on a crummock,
I wonder didna turn thy stomach.

But *Tam* kend what was what fu' brawlie,
There was ae winsome wench and wawlie,
That night enlisted in the core,
(Lang after kend on *Carrick* shore;
For mony a beast to dead she shot,
And perish'd mony a bony boat,
And shook baith meikle corn and bear,
And kept the country-side in fear:)
Her cutty sark, o' Paisley harn,
That while a lassie she had worn,
In longitude tho' sorely scanty,
It was her best, and she was vauntie. –
Ah! little kend thy reverend grannie,
That sark she coft for her wee Nannie,
Wi' twa pund Scots, ('twas a' her riches),
Wad ever grac'd a dance of witches!

But here my Muse her wing maun cour;
Sic flights are far beyond her pow'r;
To sing how Nannie lap and flang,
(A souple jade she was, and strang),
And how *Tam* stood, like ane bewitch'd,
And thought his very een enrich'd;
Even Satan glowr'd, and fidg'd fu' fain,

And hotch'd and blew wi' might and main:
Till first ae caper, syne anither,
Tam tint his reason a' thegither,
And roars out, 'Weel done, Cutty-sark!'
And in an instant all was dark;
And scarcely had he Maggie rallied,
When out the hellish legion sallied.

As bees bizz out wi' angry fyke,
When plundering herds assail their byke;
As open pussie's mortal foes,
When, pop! she starts before their nose;
As eager runs the market-crowd,
When 'Catch the thief!' resounds aloud;
So Maggie runs, the witches follow,
Wi' mony an eldritch skreech and hollow.

Ah, *Tam*! Ah, *Tam*! thou'll get thy fairin!
In hell they'll roast thee like a herrin!
In vain thy *Kate* awaits thy comin!
Kate soon will be a woefu' woman!
Now, do thy speedy utmost, Meg,
And win the key-stane of the brig;
There at them thou thy tail may toss,
A running stream they dare na cross.
But ere the key-stane she could make,
The fient a tail she had to shake!
For Nannie, far before the rest,

Hard upon noble Maggie prest,
And flew at *Tam* wi' furious ettle;
But little wist she Maggie's mettle –
Ae spring brought off her master hale,
But left behind her ain gray tail:
The carlin claught her by the rump,
And left poor Maggie scarce a stump.

Now, wha this tale o' truth shall read,
Ilk man and mother's son, take heed:
Where'er to drink you are inclin'd,
Or cutty-sarks run in your mind,
Think, ye may buy the joys o'er dear,
Remember Tam o' Shanter's mare.

The Banks o' Doon

Ye banks and braes o' bonie Doon,
    How can ye bloom sae fresh and fair;
How can ye chant, ye little birds,
    And I sae weary, fu' o' care!
Thou'll break my heart, thou warbling bird,
    That wantons thro' the flowering thorn:
Thou minds me o' departed joys,
    Departed, never to return. –

Oft hae I rov'd by bonie Doon,
    To see the rose and woodbine twine;

And ilka bird sang o' it Luve,
    And fondly sae did I o' mine. –
Wi' lightsome heart I pu'd a rose,
    Fu' sweet upon its thorny tree;
And my fause Luver staw my rose,
    But, ah! he lef the thorn wi' me. –

Lament for James, Earl of Glencairn

The wind blew hollow frae the hills,
    By fits the sun's departing beam
Look'd on the fading yellow woods
    That wav'd o'er Lugar's winding stream:
Beneath a craigy steep, a Bard,
    Laden with years and meikle pain,
In loud lament bewail'd his lord,
    Whom death had all untimely taen.

He lean'd him to an ancient aik,
    Whose trunk was mould'ring down with years;
His locks were bleached white with time,
    His hoary cheek was wet wi' tears;
And as he touch'd his trembling harp,
    And as he tuned his doleful sang,
The winds, lamenting thro' their caves,
    To echo bore the notes alang.

'Ye scatter'd birds that faintly sing,
  'The reliques of the vernal quire;
'Ye woods that shed on a' the winds
  'The honours of the aged year:
'A few short months, and glad and gay,
  'Again ye'll charm the ear and e'e;
'But nocht in all-revolting time
  'Can gladness bring again to me.

'I am a bending aged tree,
  'That long has stood the wind and rain;
'But now has come a cruel blast,
  'And my last hald of earth is gane:
'Nae leaf o' mine shall greet the spring,
  'Nae simmer sun exalt my bloom;
'But I maun lie before the storm,
  And ithers plant them in my room.

'I've seen sae mony changefu' years,
  'On earth I am a stranger grown;
'I wander in the ways of men,
  'Alike unknowing and unknown:
'Unheard, unpitied, unreliev'd,
  'I bear alane my lade o' care,
'For silent, low, on beds of dust,
  'Lie a' that would my sorrows share.

'And last, (the sum of a' my griefs!)
  'My noble master lies in clay;
'The flower amang our barons bold,
  'His country's pride, his country's stay:
'In weary being now I pine,
  'For all the life of life is dead,
'And hope has left my aged ken,
  'On forward wing for ever fled.

'Awake thy last sad voice, my harp!
  'The voice of woe and wild despair!
'Awake, resound thy latest lay,
  'Then sleep in silence evermair!
'And thou, my last, best, only friend,
  'That fillest an untimely tomb,
'Accept this tribute from the Bard
  'Thou brought from fortune's mirkest gloom.

'In Poverty's low barren vale,
  'Thick mists, obscure, involv'd me round;
'Through oft I turned the wistful eye,
  'Nae ray of fame was to be found:
'Thou found'st me, like the morning sun
  'That melts the fogs in limpid air,
'The friendless Bard and rustic song,
  'Became alike thy fostering care.

'O! why has Worth so short a date?
  'While villains ripen grey with time!

'Must thou, the noble, generous, great,
   'Fall in bold manhood's hardy prime!
'Why did I live to see that day?
   'A day to me so full of woe?
'O! had I met the mortal shaft
   'Which laid my benefactor low!

'The bridegroom may forget the bride,
   'Was made his wedded wife yestreen;
'The monarch may forget the crown
   'That on his head an hour has been;
'The mother may forget the child
   'That smiles sae sweetly on her knee;
'But I'll remember thee, Glencairn,
   'And a' that thou hast done for me!'

Song – Ae fond kiss

Ae fond kiss, and then we sever;
Ae fareweel, and then for ever!
Deep in heart-wrung tears I'll pledge thee,
Warring sighs and groans I'll wage thee. –

Who shall say that Fortune grieves him,
While the star of hope she leaves him:
Me, nae chearful twinkle lights me;
Dark despair around benights me. –

I'll ne'er blame my partial fancy,
Naething could resist my Nancy:
But to see her, was to love her;
Love but her, and love for ever. –

Had we never lov'd sae kindly,
Had we never lov'd sae blindly!
Never met – or never parted,
We had ne'er been broken-hearted. –

Fare-thee-weel, though first and fairest!
Fare-thee-weel, thou best and dearest!
Thine be ilka joy and treasure,
Peace, Enjoyment, Love and Pleasure! –

Ae fond kiss, and then we sever!
Ae fareweel, Alas, for ever!
Deep in heart-wrung tears I'll pledge thee,
Warring sighs and groans I'll wage thee. –

The De'il's awa wi' th' Exciseman

The deil cam fiddlin thro' the town,
   And danc'd awa wi' th' Exciseman;
And ilka wife cries, auld Mahoun,
   I wish you luck o' the prize, man.

The deil's awa the deil's awa
    The deil's awa wi' th' Exciseman,
He's danc'd awa he's danc'd awa
    He's danc'd awa wi' th' Exciseman.

We'll mak our maut and we'll brew our drink,
    We'll laugh, sing, and rejoice, man;
And mony braw thanks to the meikle black deil,
    That danc'd awa wi' th' Exciseman.
     The deil's awa &c.

There's threesome reels, there's foursome reels,
    There's hornpipes and strathspeys, man,
But the ae best dance e'er cam to the Land
    Was, the deil's awa wi' th' Exciseman.
     The deil's awa &c.

Highland Mary

Ye banks, and braes, and streams around
    The castle o' Montgomery,
Green be your woods, and fair your flowers,
    Your waters never drumlie!
There Simmer first unfald her robes,
    And there the largest tarry:
For there I took the last Fareweel
    O' my sweet Highland Mary.

How sweetly bloom'd the gay, green birk,
　　How rich the hawthorn's blossom;
As underneath their fragrant shade,
　　I clasp'd her to my bosom!
The golden Hours, on angel wings,
　　Flew o'er me and my Dearie;
For dear to me as light and life
　　Was my sweet Highland Mary.

Wi' mony a vow, and lock'd embrace,
　　Our parting was fu' tender;
And pledging aft to meet again,
　　We tore oursels asunder:
But Oh, fell Death's untimely frost,
　　That nipt my Flower sae early!
Now green's the sod, and cauld's the clay,
　　That wraps my Highland Mary!

O pale, pale now, those rosy lips
　　I aft hae kiss'd sae fondly!
And clos'd for ay, the sparkling glance,
　　That dwalt on me sae kindly!
And mouldering now in silent dust,
　　That heart that lo'ed me dearly!
But still within my bosom's core
　　Shall live my Highland Mary.

Duncan Gray

Duncan Gray cam here to woo,
    Ha, ha, the wooing o't,
On blythe Yule night when we were fu',
    Ha, ha, the wooing o't.
Maggie coost her head fu' high,
Look'd asklent and unco skiegh,
Gart poor Duncan stand abiegh;
    Ha, ha, the wooing o't.

Duncan fleech'd, and Duncan pray'd;
    Ha, ha the wooing o't.
Meg was deaf as Ailsa craig,
    Ha, ha, the wooing o't.
Duncan sigh'd baith out and in,
Grat his een baith bleer't an' blin',
Spak o' lowpin o'er a linn;
    Ha, ha, the wooing o't.

Time and Chance are but a tide;
    Ha, ha, the wooing o't.
Slighted love is sair to bide,
    Ha, ha, the wooing o't.
Shall I, like a fool, quoth he,
For a haughty hizzie die?
She may gae to – France for me!
    Ha, ha, the wooing o't.

How it comes let Doctors tell,
    Ha, ha, the wooing o't.
Meg grew sick as he grew heal,
    Ha, ha, the wooing o't.
Something in her bosom wrings,
For relief a sigh she brings;
And O her een, they spak sic things!
    Ha, ha, the wooing o't.

Duncan was a lad o' grace,
    Ha, ha, the wooing o't.
Maggie's was a piteous case,
    Ha, ha, the wooing o't.
Duncan could na be her death,
Swelling Pity smoor'd his Wrath;
Now they're crouse and canty baith,
    Ha, ha, the wooing o't.

Phillis the fair –

While larks with little wing
    Fann'd the pure air,
Viewing the breathing spring,
    Forth I did fare:
Gay the sun's golden eye
Peep'd o'er the mountains high;
Such thy morn! did I cry,
    Phillis the fair.

In each bird's careless song,
   Glad, I did share;
While yon wild flowers among
   Chance led me there:
Sweet to the opening day,
Rosebuds bent the dewy spray;
Such thy bloom, did I say,
   Phillis the fair.

Down in a shady walk,
   Doves cooing were;
I mark'd the cruel hawk,
   Caught in a snare:
So kind may Fortune be,
Such make his destiny!
He who would injure thee,
   Phillis the fair.

Robert Bruce's March to Bannockburn –

Scots, wha hae wi' WALLACE bled,
Scots, wham BRUCE has aften led,
Welcome to your gory bed, –
   Or to victorie. –

Now 's the day, and now 's the hour;
See the front o' battle lour;
See approach proud EDWARD's power,
   Chains and Slaverie. –

Wha will be a traitor-knave?
Wha can fill a coward's grave?
Wha sae base as be a Slave?
   – Let him turn and flie:–

Wha for SCOTLAND's king and law,
Freedom's sword will strongly draw,
FREE-MAN stand, or FREE-MAN fa',
   Let him follow me. –

By Oppression's woes and pains!
By your Sons in servile chains!
We will drain our dearest veins,
   But they *shall* be free!

Lay the proud Usurpers low!
Tyrants fall in every foe!
LIBERTY's in every blow!
   Let us DO – OR DIE!!!

A red red Rose

O my Luve 's like a red, red rose,
   That's newly sprung in June;

O my Luve 's like the melodie
   That 's sweetly play'd in tune. –

As fair art thou, my bonie lass,
   So deep in luve am I;
And I will love thee still, my Dear,
   Till a' the seas gang dry. –

Till a' the seas gang dry, my Dear,
   And the rocks melt wi' the sun:
I will love thee still, my Dear,
   While the sands o' life shall run. –

And fare thee weel, my only Luve!
   And fare thee weel, a while!
And I will come again, my Luve,
   Tho' it were ten thousand mile!

Song – For a' that and a' that –

Is there, for honest Poverty
   That hings his head, and a' that;
That coward-slave, we pass him by,
   We dare be poor for a' that!
For a' that, and a' that,

Our toils obscure, and a' that,
The rank is but the guinea's stamp,
    The Man 's the gowd for a' that. –

What though on hamely fare we dine,
    Wear hoddin grey, and a' that.
Gie fools their silks, and knaves their wine,
    A man 's a Man for a' that.
    For a' that, and a' that,
        Their tinsel show, and a' that;
The honest man, though e'er sae poor,
    Is king o' men for a' that. –

Ye see yon birkie ca'd, a lord,
    Wha struts, and stares, and a' that,
Though hundreds worship at his word,
    He's but a coof for a' that.
    For a' that, and a' that,
        His ribband, star and a' that,
The man of independent mind,
    He looks and laughs at a' that. –

A prince can mak a belted knight,
    A marquis, duke, and a' that;
But an honest man's aboon his might,
    Gude faith he mauna fa' that!
    For a' that, and a' that,
        Their dignities, and a' that,

The pith o' Sense, and pride o' Worth,
    Are higher rank that a' that. –

Then let us pray that come it may,
    As come it will for a' that,
That Sense and Worth, o'er a' the earth
    Shall bear the gree, and a' that.
    For a' that, and a' that,
    That Man to Man the warld o'er,
    Shall brothers be for a' that. –

Comin thro' the rye

Comin thro' the rye, poor body,
    Comin thro' the rye,
She draigl't a' her petticoatie
    Comin thro' the rye.
    Oh Jenny's a' weet, poor body,
        Jenny's seldom dry;
      She draigl't a' her petticoatie
        Comin thro' the rye.

Gin a body meet a body
    Comin' thro' the rye,
Gin a body kiss a body
    Need a body cry.
      Oh Jenny's a' weet, &c.

Gin a body meet a body
  Comin thro' he glen;
Gin a body kiss a body
  Need the warld ken!
    Oh Jenny's a' weet, &c.

Charlie he's my darling

'Twas on a monday morning,
  Right early in the year,
That Charlie cam to our town,
  The young Chevalier. –

CHORUS
An' Charlie he's my darling, my darling, my darling,
Charlie he's my darling, the young Chevalier. –

As he was walking up the street,
  The city for to view,
O there he spied a bonie lass
  The window looking thro'. –
    An Charlie &c.

Sae light 's he jimped up the stair,
  And tirled at the pin;
And wha sae ready as hersel

To let the laddie in. –
    An Charlie &c.

He set his Jenny on his knee,
    All in his Highland dress;
For brawlie weel he ken'd the way
    To please a bonie lass. –
      An Charlie &c.

Its up yon hethery mountain,
    And down yon scroggy glen,
We daur na gang a milking,
    For Charlie and his men. –
      An Charlie &c.

For the sake o' Somebody –

My heart is sair, I dare na tell,
    My heart is sair for Somebody;
I could wake a winter-night
    For the sake o' Somebody. –
      Oh-hon! for Somebody!
      Oh-hey! for Somebody!
I could range the warld round,
    For the sake o' Somebody. –

Ye Powers that smile on virtuous love,
    O, sweetly smile on Somebody!

53

Frae ilka danger keep him free,
    And send me safe my Somebody. –
    Ohon! for Somebody!
    Ohey! for Somebody!
I wad do – what was I not –
    For the sake o' Somebody!

The Selkirk Grace

Some hae meat, and canna eat,
    And some wad eat that want it;
But we hae meat and we can eat,
    And sae the Lord be thanket.

A Note on Robert Burns

Robert Burns (1759–96), Scottish poet, born at Alloway, near Ayr, in a cottage built by his father, a farmer from Kincardineshire who spelt his name Burnes. The careful instruction that Burns had from him and from John Murdoch, the village schoolmaster, disposes of the theory that he was inspired but illiterate. His father, who tried constantly but without success to better his position, took a farm in 1765 at Mount Oliphant. At 16 Burns had some additional though intermittent schooling, and managed to learn from Murdoch the rudiments of French. His first song, 'Handsome Nell', was written when he was 16, inspired by a young partner at the harvesting. In a brief visit to a school at Kirkoswald, 1775, he learned surveying; and during this period he made friends to whom he later addressed poetry. In 1777 the family moved to Lochlie in the parish of Tarbolton, but their farm there failed in 1783. Burns had gone to Irvine in 1781 to learn the trade of flax-dressing, but that project ended when the shop was burned down during a Hogmanay celebration. Finally, in 1784, when his father died of consumption, Robert and his brother Gilbert invested what little capital could be saved in the farm of Mossgiel near Mauchline.

Mossgiel proved no more successful than their other ventures, and meanwhile Burns had fallen in love with Jean Armour, daughter of a master mason. Separation followed a quarrel with her family, and Burns, considering himself free again, decided, as a desperate bid for fortune, to emigrate to Jamaica as bookkeeper on a plantation. He intended that Mary Campbell should accompany him to Jamaica as his wife, but she died. Burns later commemorated his romance in several poems, including the famous 'Highland Mary'. New circumstances then entirely changed his plans. To get money for his passage he published *Poems Chiefly in the Scottish Dialect*, 1786 (the famous 'Kilmarnock Burns'), which was an immediate success. It contained much of his best work, especially in social criticism, including 'The Twa Dogs', 'Hallowe'en', 'The Holy Fair', 'To a Mouse', 'To a Mountain Daisy', and 'The Cotter's Saturday Night'. On seeing the collection Dr Thomas Blacklock dissuaded Burns from going abroad, and arrangements were made for an Edinburgh edition of the poems, 1787. This eventually brought him £500, but at the cost of losing the copyright. In Edinburgh Burns was received on friendly terms by Dugald Stewart, the philosopher, William Robertson, the historian, and Hugh Blair, the critic, as well as by such aristocrats as the Earl of Glencairn.

Always a good conversationalist, he made a favourable

impression by his frankness and modesty, and formed friendships with, among others, Mrs McLehose, the 'Clarinda' of his letters, and Mrs Dunlop of Dunlop, with whom he also corresponded for a time. Walter Scott, then a boy of 15, saw him and described him later as 'of manners rustic, not clownish' ... 'the eye alone indicated the poetical character and temperament. It was large and of a dark cast, and literally glowed when he spoke with feeling or interest'. In August 1788 Burns married Jean Armour, used his capital to try a new farm, Ellisland, on the banks of the Nith near Dumfries, and learned the duties of an exciseman.

At Ellisland he was cultivated by the local gentry, and it was suggested that he should be a candidate for the newly founded chair of agriculture at Edinburgh University, but he declined. This farm also proving unsatisfactory, in 1791 he moved to Dumfries and became a full-time gauger or exciseman. The advantages of a steady income, however, were partly offset by the opportunities for hard drinking, which had long been his weakness. Meanwhile he began one of his most important literary tasks, the provision of songs for the *Scots Musical Museum* compiled by James Johnson, 1787–1803, and also for George Thomson's *Select Collection of Original Scottish Airs*. Burns's contribution of over 300 songs, many of his own composition, many based on older verses or fitted to old tunes, is perhaps his supreme achievement. It was entirely a labour of love, for he received no payment. At this time also he wrote in one day the rollicking 'Tam o'Shanter', reckoned the greatest of his longer poems. In 1792 he nearly lost his job because of his radical opinions, but he kept his post, and looked forward confidently to a supervisorship. His prospects had never seemed brighter when in 1796 he died of endocarditis, following an attack of rheumatism.

Burns is recognised as the culminating figure in two centuries' tradition of folk-song and genre poetry and one of the greatest of all writers of love songs. Whether composing original pieces or, as in the case of 'Auld Lang Syne', revitalising a song which had already passed through more than one version, he had the sure touch of lyric genius. To this he added a power of vitriolic satire shown in such poems as 'Holy Willie's Prayer', and a command of vivid description that appears at its best in 'Tam o'Shanter' and 'The Jolly Beggars'. His poetry owed much to Allan Ramsay and to Robert Fergusson, who stands in much the same relation to Burns as Marlowe to Shakespeare; but he far surpassed both his Scottish forerunners, and, though not a Romantic himself, the example of his work was one of the vital influences in the coming Romantic Movement. His strength lies in his essential sincerity to his own experience and the extraordinary vitality of its expression.

Other titles in this series

ANDREW MARVELL   *To His Coy Mistress*
JOHN MILTON   *Paradise Lost*
WILFRED OWEN   *The Pity of War*
PALGRAVE   *Golden Treasury of Love Poems*
EDGAR ALLAN POE   *The Raven*
ALEXANDER POPE   *The Rape of the Lock*
CHRISTINA ROSSETTI   *Goblin Market*
SIR WALTER SCOTT   *Lochinvar*
WILLIAM SHAKESPEARE   *Love Sonnets*
PERCY BYSSHE SHELLEY   *To a Skylark*
EDMUND SPENSER   *The Fairy Queen*
ALFRED, LORD TENNYSON   *The Lady of Shalott*
DYLAN THOMAS   *Fern Hill*
EDWARD THOMAS   *There Was a Time*
R. S. THOMAS   *Love Poems*
FRANCIS THOMPSON   *The Hound of Heaven*
WALT WHITMAN   *I Sing the Body Electric*
WILLIAM WORDSWORTH   *Intimations of Immortality*
W. B. YEATS   *Sailing to Byzantium*